Diet recommendations during TCM - Lung - Phlegm Cold

Please check these recommendations always with a nutrition consultant, therapist, doctor or dietician. The recipes and the list of ingredients are supporting the conventional medical therapy. The calorie disclosures of fresh ingredients (fruit and vegetables) vary according to quality and time of harvest. The contents were checked by a dietician and a nutrition consultant for the Traditional Chinese Medicine (TCM).

Author:
©2020 Josef Miligui
www.ebns.at

Source:
The lists are created from the EBNS database for nutritional counseling. The database is used by dietitians, therapists and doctors for advising the patient / client.

Literature:
The specialist literature and the training documents of the German and Austrian dietary and traditional Chinese medicine serve as a knowledge base. We have used the documents as a basis of knowledge, adapted it to our experience and completed them.
http://nutribook.info/

Production and publishing:
BoD – Books on Demand, Norderstedt
ISBN: 9783750414099

Diet recommendations for TCM - Lung - Phlegm Cold

1 Treatment strategy 3
2 Avoid 3
3 Recipes 3
    3.1   Cooling rice dish with grapefruit 3
    3.2   Japanese algae soup 4
    3.3   Oat Congee 5
    3.4   Spicy Tofu Vegetable Pan 5
    3.5   Tea from thyme 6
4 Effects of food 6
    4.1   Use ingredients: recommendable 6
    4.2   Use ingredients: yes 7
    4.3   Use ingredients: little 7
    4.4   Do not use contra-acting foods 7
5 Complementary 11
    5.1   Fennel 11
    5.2   Ginger fresh 12
    5.3   Sage 12
    5.4   Summer savory 13
6 Basics of Nutrition 14
    6.1   Nutrition 14
    6.2   Recipes 16
    6.3   Foodstuffs 16
    6.4   Herbs 17
7 Other dietic-books 18
8 EBNS - Software for nutritional counseling 20

1 Treatment strategy

Release mucus, lower lungs, tone spleen, calm cough.
avoid cold / refreshing - more warming food.

2 Avoid

Bad diet style, cold drinks, no meat 4 hours before sleep, too much bread, cereals, too much raw food, cold foods / drinks, dairy products, tropical fruits, fruit juices, denatured food, factory sugar, fried, breaded and fat.
See also damp cold in the spleen.

3 Recipes

(rec.) = You can use more.
(little) = You should use less than specified
(omit) = omit.

3.1 Cooling rice dish with grapefruit

Lowers lung Qi, nourishes fluids, dissolves mucus, dries out, passes downwardly, warms the stomach and spleen, harmonizes the intestine, forces Qi, reduces moisture, strengthens Qi and Kidney Jing, moisturizes, relaxes, builds up Qi, spreads.
Cooking time approx. 20 min
Calories p. portion: 234
4 portions
Allergens: GHO

Quantity of ingredients
Rice round grain 1 cup / 120g. (yes) - neutral - sweet .... metal
Water 5 cups / 600g. (yes) - cool - salty .... earth
Hazelnuts 2 table spoons / 20g. () - neutral - sweet .... earth
Raisins 2 table spoons / 20g. () - warm - sweet .... earth
Agave nectar 1 table spoon / 10g. () - cool - sweet .... *
Salt 1 pinch / 0,2g. (little) - cold - salty .... water
Almond puree 1 table spoon / 10g. () - neutral - sweet .... earth
Grapefruit (Pomelo) 1 piece / 200g. (rec.) - cool - sweet, sour .... fire
Butter organic 2 teaspoons / 20g. (yes) - neutral - sweet .... earth

Cooking instructions:
Preparation on the eve: Pour round grain rice into cold water and cook. Soak chopped hazelnuts and raisins in some hot water overnight.

In the morning: Stir in a little hot water some agave syrup; add the rice and heat; add a small pinch of salt, almond paste, chopped grapefruit, the soaked chopped hazelnuts and raisins and mix; Serve with a small piece of butter.

3.2 Japanese algae soup

Strengthens spleen and liver, regulates Qi flow, moisturizes, relaxes, builds up Qi, spreads, nourishes the lungs and spleen, distributes mucus, dissolves mucus, dissolves stagnation, directs upwards, gets Qi moving und Yang.
Cooking time approx. 20 min
Calories p. portion: 47
3 portions

Quantity of ingredients
Wakame 1 oz / 25g. () - cold - salty..water
Water 2 cup / 450g. (yes) - cool - salty......................................earth
Onion (shallot) 1-2 pcs. / 30g. (yes) - warm - acrid, sweet.......................metal
Radish (white, green, purple-red) 1/8 lbs - 2oz / 50g. (yes) - cool - sweet, acrid
  metal
Carrot 2 pieces / 180g. (yes) - neutral - sweet ....earth
Miso 2 table spoons / 20g. (yes) - neutral - salty......................................water
Parsley 2 table spoons / 20g. () - warm - bitter ....wood
Onion (spring onion) 1 table spoon (sliced)...metal

Cooking instructions:
Soak wakame in water for a few minutes, remove and bring the water to the boil. Add finely chopped onions and wakame, radishes and carrots, cut into thin strips, and simmer for another 10 minutes. Dissolve miso in a little cooled cooking water and add it at the end. Sprinkle with parsley and spring onions.

3.3   Oat Congee

Forces Qi, forces liver and spleen, moisturizes intestines, eliminates mucus, holds back sweat.
Cooking time approx. 2-4 hours
Calories p. portion: 162
3 portions
Allergens: A

Quantity of ingredients
Oat 1 cup / 125g. (yes) - warm - sweet .... metal
Water 6 cups / 700g. (yes) - cool - salty.. earth

Cooking instructions:
Cook oats and water in a ratio of about 1: 6. The amount of water determines the thickness of the mash (pure matter of taste). The oats swell, so do not take much. Put the oats in a saucepan with good insulation and a heavy lid. It is important to simmer the oats after a short boil on the slightest flame, otherwise it burns. Cook the oat for 2-4 hours. The longer it cooks, the more he strengthens.

3.4   Spicy Tofu Vegetable Pan

Nourishing and slightly refreshing, builds up Qi and fluids, regulates Qi, warms the inside, lowers cold, forces stomach, relieves constipation, forces Yang, Dissolves mucus, reduces wind.
Cooking time approx. 25 min
Calories p. portion: 241
4 portions
Allergens: EN

Quantity of ingredients
Sesame oil 2 table spoons / 20g. () - cool - sweet .... earth
Carrot 2 pieces / 100g. (yes) - neutral - sweet .... earth
Fennel 1 piece / 250g. (yes) - warm - sweet, little acrid .... earth
Leek 1 piece / 200g. (yes) - warm - acrid .... metal
Salt 1 pinch / 1g. (little) - cold - salty .... water
Turmeric (yellow root) 1 pinch / 1g. (yes) - warm - bitter................................*
Lemon juice 1 dash / 1g. () - cold - sour.. wood
Soy Tofu 1 package / 120g. (yes) - cool - sweet .... earth
Pepper (ground) 1 pinch / 0,5g. () - warm - acrid .... metal
Soy sauce 1 dash / 3g. () - cold - salty .... water
Rice (whole grain) 1 cup / 120g. () - warm - sweet..................................... metal
Water 6 cups / 500g. (yes) - cool - salty... earth
Salt 1 pinch / 1g. (little) - cold - salty .... water

Cooking instructions:
Heat sesame oil in a hot wok or a hot pan; fry the chopped carrots, fennel and leek slices; salt, a dash of lemon juice, turmeric, tofu cubes roast for 1 - 2 minutes.
Add the pepper and cook covered for about 5 minutes; drizzle with soy sauce.
Place the rice in salted water, heat till it boils and let it simmer over low heat for about 15 minutes.

3.5   Tea from thyme

Converts mucus, forces lungs and spleen, dries out, passes downwardly.
Cooking time approx. 10 min
Calories p. portion: 0
4 portions

Quantity of ingredients
Thyme 3 table spoons / 6g. (rec.) - warm - bitter .... *
Water 2 cup water / 500g. (yes) - cool - salty .... earth

Cooking instructions:
Heat the water till it boils and put it aside. Add thyme and 10 min. to let go. Strain. Sweet to taste with honey.
Drink 2 to 3 cups daily.

4   Effects of food

4.1   Use ingredients: recommendable

Adzuki beans
Basil
Basil (fresh)
Bitter orange peel
Black caraway
Champignon
Chenpi (chinese tangerine bowl)
Coix (seeds) YiYi Ren
Ginger fresh

Grapefruit (Pomelo)
Grapefruit juice
Ground
Kumquats
Marjoram
Orange grated peel
Oregano dried
Reishi mushroom
Thyme

4.2 Use ingredients: yes

Barley
Barley not peeled
Basic recipe for a fish soup
Basic recipe for a vegetable soup
(nutritious)
Boxhorn clover seeds
Butter organic
Carrot
Carrot (Early Carrot)
Carrot juice without sugar
Celery root
Celery sticks
Cereal coffee
Chinese cabbage
Cress
Fennel
Ginger powder
Leek
Miso
Oat
Olive oil

Onion (shallot)
Onion (spring onion)
Onion read
Onion white
Parsley root
Parsnip
Peas, green
Radish
Radish (white, green, purple-red)
Radish black
Rice Basmati
Rice long grain rice
Rice round grain
Savory
Soy Tofu
Tsampa (roasted barley flour)
Turmeric (yellow root)
Turnips
Water
Water hot
Zucchini

4.3 Use ingredients: little

Apple (sour)
Apple (sweet)
Beef fillet
Beef meat
Beef meat (calf)
Black beans
Breadcrumbs (wheat bread, bread roll)
Broad beans (thick beans)
Broccoli
Brussels sprouts
Bush beans
Butter beans white
Cauliflower
French beans

Grape juice red
Grape juice white
Kidney beans (red)
Kohlrabi
Lima beans
Multi-grain bread (gray bread)
Pinto beans speckled
Red cabbage
Salt
Savoy cabbage / kale
White beans
White bread (wheat bread)
White cabbage

4.4 Do not use contra-acting foods

Agar agar (kelp)
Almond
Almond marzipan
Almond milk
Almond puree
Aloe juice
Amaranth
Anchovy / Sardine
Anise (Common Fennel)
Apricot
Apricots

Arrowroot
Artichoke
Asparagus (green or white)
Aubergino
Avocado
Balm
Bamboo shoots
Banana
Banana (cooking banana)
Barley malt
Basic recipe for a beef soup (warming)

Basic recipe for a chicken soup (warming)
Basic recipe for a duck soup
Basic recipe for a rice soup (Congee)
Batavia
Bean oil
Beef bone marrow
Beef heart
Beef kidney
Beef liver
Beef meatbones
Beef stomach
Beer (Pils)
Beer (Top-fermented German dark beer)
Berry juice
Bitter Herb liqueur
Bitter melon
Black tea
Blackberry´s
Black-eyed peas
Blueberry
Blueberry juice
Bocksdorn fruits (Fructus Lycii, Goji, goji berry
Boletus mushroom
Borage
Borage oil
Brown ale
Buckwheat
Bulgur (cereals)
Burdock root tea
Buttermilk
Calamari
Cantaloupe
Capers in olive oil
Carambola (Star fruit)
Carp
Cashews
Caviar
Channa-Dal
Chanterelle
Chard
Cherry
Cherry juice
Chervil
Chestnuts
Chicken egg
Chicken heart
Chicken liver
Chicken meat
Chicken stomach
Chicken yolk
Chickpeas

Chickweed
Chicory
Chili (pod or ground)
Chives
Chlorella (fresh water)
Chrysanthemum blossom tea
Cinnamon ground
Cinnamon sticks
Clementines
Clove
Cocoa
Coconut fat
Coconut flakes
Coconut grated
Coconut milk
Cod
Coffee
Cooking oil
Coriander
Coriander (fresh)
Corn
Corn (roasted)
Corn Grease (Polenta)
Corn silk tea
Couscous
Cow's milk (1.5% fat)
Cow's milk (whole milk 3.5% fat)
Crab
Cranberry
Cranberry juice
Cream, sweet 30%
Créme fraiche cheese
Crucian
Cucumber
Cumin (Caraway seed)
Curcuma
Curd cheese 20%
Curd cheese 40%
Currant (black)
Currant (red)
Currant (white)
Curry
Curry paste red
Daisy
Dandelion (young plants)
Dandelion juice
Dandelionroots tea
Dates dried
Dates red
Deer meat
Deer meat
Dill
Duck (heart)
Duck (slaughtered)

Dulse (seaweed)
Eel
Elderberry blossom tee
Endive salad
Evening primrose oil
Fennel seeds ground
Fennel tea
Feta cheese
Fig
Fig dried
Fish pieces mixed (fresh water)
Fish remains
Flower pollen
Fresh cheese
Freshwater fish
Fruit tea
Galangal
Garlic
Gelee Royal
Gentian root
Ginger oil
Goat
Goat and sheep's milk
Goat cheese
Goose
Goose egg
Goose parts
Gooseberry
Gourd
Grapefruit dried peel
Grapes red
Grapes white
Grass carp
Green spelt
Green tea
Ground caraway
Hawthorn
Hazelnuts
Herbs bitter
Herbs of Provence
Herbs various
Herbs wild
Herring
Hibiscus
Honey
Hyssop
Iceberg lettuce
Jasmine blossoms tee
Juniper berry
Kefir
Kiwi
Kombu seaweed (Saccharina japonica)
Kukicha tea
Lamb bones

Lamb kidneys
Lamb liver
Lamb meat
Lamb shoulder
Lamb's lettuce
Leaf salads (bitter)
Lemon
Lemon juice
Lemon peel
Lemongrass
Lentils
Lentils black
Lentils red
Lentils yellow
Lettuce
Licorice root tea
Lime
Lime blossom tea
Linseed oil
Lobster
Longane
Lovage
Lychee
Lychee in Preserved
Mackerel
Mallow (Malva sylvestris) blossom tea
Malt
Mango
Maple syrup
Margarine
Margarine (diet)
Mediterranean fish (cod, plaice, haddock, sea
Millet
Millet flakes
Mineral water
Mirabelle plum
Miso paste (soy bean paste)
Mold cheese
Morel (black, dried)
Morel, dried
Mozzarella
Mulberry fruit
Mulled Wine Spice
Mullet
Mung bean
Mung bean sprouting
Mussels
Mustard
Mustard seeds
Mustard sweet
Mutton
Mutton
Nutmeg

Oat flakes (whole grain)
Oat flakes roasted
Oat flour
Oat fusion (baby food)
Oat meal
Octopus
Okra
Olives
Orange
Orange juice
Oyster mushroom
Oyster shell powder
Oysters
Papaya
Parmesan
Parsley
Passion blossoms tea
Peaches
Peaches (canned)
Peanut oil
Peanuts
Pear
Pear juice
Pearl barley
Peas
Pepper Cayenne
Pepper white (ground)
Peppercorns
Peppermint
Pepperoni, red, pitted, halved
Peppers
Peppers (rose peppers)
Peppers (sweet)
Perch
Pheasant
Pickle
Pigeon
Pimento
Pine nuts
Pineapple
Pineapple (from a can)
Pineapple juice without sugar
Pistachios
Plaice
Plum
Plums
Pomegranate
Poppy
Pork heart
Pork knuckle
Pork liver
Pork meat
Pork skin
Pork stomach

Potato
Pumpkin
Pumpkin seed oil
Pumpkin seeds
Quail
Quail egg
Quince
Quinoa
Rabbit
Rabbit liver
Rabbit meat
Radicchio
Radish horseradish
Radish leaves
Raisins
Rapeseed oil
Raspberry
Raspberry dried (immature)
Red berry (without sugar)
Red wine
Rhubarb
Rice (fragrance)
Rice (whole grain)
Rice black
Rice flour
Rice malt
Rice noodles
Rice red
Rice sweet
Rice variety any
Rice wild (nature rice)
Romaine lettuce / lettuce salad
Rose hip tea
Rose leaf tea
Rosefish
Rosemary
Rye
Rye flour
Safflower (Dyer's thistle / Hong Hua)
Saffron
Sage
Sago (cereals)
Sake
Salmon
Salsify
Sauerkraut (cutted cabbage fermented)
Sea buckthorn
Seacrab
Sesame oil
Sesame paste (Tahini)
Sesame, black
Sesame, white
Shark
Sheep's milk

Shiitake, dried
Shrimp
Shrimps
Sorrel
Sour cherries
Sour cream 15% fat
Sour milk
Sour milk cheese 20%
Sourdough
Soy flour
Soy sauce
Soya Cuisine (soy cream)
Soybean milk
Soybean oil
Soybeans
Soybeans, black
Soybeans, yellow
Spelled (Dark) bread
Spelled flakes
Spelled grain
Spelled semolina
Spelled wholemeal flour
Spinach
Spiny lobsters
Spirit
Star anise
Strawberries
Strawberry Juice
Sugar brown
Sugar candy white
Sugar cane sugar
Sugar fructose - fruit sugar
Sugar glucose - grapes sugar
Sugar Milk Sugar
Sugar molasses
Sugar white
Sunflower oil
Sunflower seeds
Sweet potato

Tangerine
Tarragon (Estragon)
Thistle oil
Tomato
Tomato dried
Trout
Tuna
Turkey breast meat
Umeboshi plums (Japanese apricots)
Vanilla
Vanilla powder
Vegetable juice
Vinegar (Apple vinegar)
Vinegar (Red wine vinegar)
Vinegar Aceto Balsamico
Wakame
Walnut oil
Walnuts
Walnuts roasted
Watermelon
Wheat
Wheat beer
Wheat bran
Wheat bulgur
Wheat flakes
Wheat flour
Wheat germ oil
Wheat semolina
Wheat semolina for children
Wheatgrass juice
White wine
Wild boar meat
Wild strawberries
Wormwood
Yarrow tea
Yeast
Yogi tea
Yogurt (natural, 1.5% fat)
Yogurt (natural, 3.5% fat)

5   Complementary

5.1   Fennel

Foeniculum vulgare
preparation: Healing tea (infusion)
Strengthens the stomach energy, warms kidney energy and has an energizing effect.
Pour 3 5 grams of tea over with 250 ml of boiling water and leave for 10 minutes. Then sieve. Drink in three doses on an empty stomach.

For the powder, roast the fennel in a dry pan until it starts to smell, then grind it to a fine powder in a mortar or food processor; Add 1-5 g powder with boiling water and drink daily.

Special Features: Fennel is one of the best remedy for physical weakness and lack of vitality due to inadequate or cold digestive energy that prevents that the body absorbs enough nutrients and energy from food.

In rare cases, skin, stomach and intestinal reactions were observed. Active ingredients: essential oil, trans-anethole, fenchone, fatty oil, protein, sugar.

5.2   Ginger fresh

Zingiberis officinalis, Rhizoma
preparation: Decoction
Strengthens juices production, reduces cold-nuisance, stimulates, stimulates the Yang-energy, warms the lung- and stomach-energy.
Put 1-6 slices of fresh root in a jug of water for 3 minutes. Drink 10 g in two doses on empty stomach.
To improve the taste is brown raw sugar
Special features: In TCM, the fresh ginger root is mainly used against fish poisoning and colds of the lungs and stomach.
Because ginger promotes nutrient uptake, it is often used in a variety of formulations to facilitate the rapid absorption of other herbs and thereby enhance their effects. Ginger contains the digestive enzyme zingibain. The digestive effect of this substance is stronger than that of the enzyme papain.
In too large quantities, ginger leads to constipation, Not to use in: pregnancy, high fever.

5.3   Sage

Salvia
preparation: Healing tea (infusion)
Expels Mucus, Dries, Guides Down, Activates Wei Qi, Strengthens Qi.
Äth. Oils containing many bitter substances and tannins should not be overdosed in order not to pollute the stomach.
Do not use on: Pregnancy

5.4 Summer savory

Satureja hortensis
preparation: Healing tea (infusion)
Tonifies kidney-yang, heart-qi, stomach- and spleen-qi and warms the middle, moves the liver-qi and blood, releases mucous and cold from the lungs, opens the surface, induces wind-cold.
Pour 2 teaspoons of the tea into 250 ml of boiling water and leave for 10 minutes. Then sieve. Drink 2 to 3 cups per day as needed. (on www.ebns.at in the shop)
The herb with the peppery aroma makes hearty dishes wholesome, has a stomach-strengthening and antibacterial, soothing and appetizing.

Ideal for preventing colds: strengthens the defense when drinking tea for 14 days. After enjoying raw food savory activates the spleen yang.
Use: in legumes, soups, salads and as a tea (not in the evening), external use: softening and anti-inflammatory, in incontinence or nocturnal wetting (but not in children), for libido the savory in schnapps insert
The herb with the peppery aroma makes hearty dishes wholesome, has a stomach-strengthening and antibacterial, soothing and appetizing.

6 Basics of Nutrition

The basic principles of nutrition described herein are general recommendations. They are not aimed at a specific form of therapy. Recommendations concerning a therapy have priority.

6.1 Nutrition

Regular meals in a relaxed atmosphere. A warm breakfast is considered a good start into the day.

The main meals ought to be taken for lunch – supper in the early evening. Pay attention to feeling hungry or sated: don't eat too much nor remain hungry is the rule

Prepare the meals freshly from natural, regional products. Frozen, heat-conserved, industrially prepared or foodstuffs cooked in the microwave oven are rejected.

Choice of foodstuffs according to the season: more cooling food in summer, more warming food in winter.

Eat cooked food at least twice a day. Food and drinks ought to be lukewarm, never ice-cold or hot.

Raw vegetables, briefly cooked vegetables, freshly squeezed juices and mineral water are not recommended. Milk and dairy products are only included in the diet if they don't cause problems. Don't use therapeutic recipes over a longer period without consulting your doctor or therapist.

Varied food

Enjoy the diversity of foodstuffs. Characteristics of a balanced nutrition are variety, suitable combination and a balanced quantity of rich and low energy foodstuffs (on one hand avoiding undersupply with essential nutrients and on the other hand to take to many undesirable substances)

A lot of Cereal Products - and Potatoes

Bread, pasta, rice, cereal flakes (best wholemeal) as well as potatoes contain almost no fat, but many vitamins, mineral nutrients, trace elements, roughage and secondary plant substances. These foodstuffs ought to be taken with low-fat side dishes.

Vegetables and Fruit – „Take Five" every day ... 5 portions of

vegetables and fruit a day, as fresh as possible, briefly cooked, or maybe one portion as a juice – ideal as a side dish to every meal as well as snack between meals: Thus a lot of vitamins, mineral nutrients as well as roughage and secondary plant substances

Daily milk and dairy products
Milk and Dairy Products every Day, once or twice per Week Fish; meat, sausages as well as eggs moderately. These foodstuffs contain valuable nutrients like calcium in the milk, iodine selenium and omega-3 fat acids in saltwater fish. Meat is favorable due to its high content of disposable iron and the vitamins B1, B6 and B12. Quantities of 300 – 600 g meat and sausage per week are sufficient. Prefer low-fat products, especially in meat- and dairy products.

Low-fat and fatty Foodstuffs
Fat supplies us with essential fat acids and fatty foodstuffs contain also fat-soluble vitamins. Fat is high in energy; therefore much fat in the food may cause overweight, possibly also cancer. Too many saturated fat acids may further a tendency for cardio-vascular diseases in the long term. Prefer vegetable oils and fats (e.g. rapeseed-, olive-, soya-oils and solid fats produced therefrom). Beware of invisible fat in meat- and dairy products, pastry and sweets as well as in fast-food and convenience foods. 70 – 90 g fat per day is sufficient.

Moderately Sugar and Salt
Take sugar and foods/drinks containing various kinds of sugar (e.g. glucose syrup) only occasionally. Use herbs and spices as well as a little salt creatively. Prefer salt containing iodine.

Plenty of Liquids
Water is absolutely essential. Drink 1-2 l liquids every day. Prefer water (with or without gas) and other low-calorie drinks. Alcoholic drinks should not be taken.

Tasty Dishes, carefully cooked
Cook the meals with as low temperatures and as short as possible, using little water and fat – this preserves the original taste, keeps the nutrients intact and prevents the production of harmful compounds.

Take time and enjoy the food
Take your Time and enjoy your Food
Eating consciously helps to eat right. The eye enjoys food, too. It's fun, invites to enjoy varied dishes and stimulates the feeling of satiety.

Watch your Weight and stay in Motion
A balanced diet and a lot of exercise and sport (30 – 60 min/day) are a healthy combination. The right weight furthers well-being and health.

Thermals, directional effectiveness, digestive power
There are various criteria for judging the effectiveness of herbs and foodstuffs.
The use of certain herbs and ingredients is based on observations of the effects on the body which these foodstuffs, herbs and spices show after having eaten them. The medical science has developed following system Every ingredient or herb has a directional effectiveness. Furthermore, there are herbs which have a special effect on certain organs.
The basic condition for a healthy metabolism is to obtain sufficient energy from food and that the digestive process doesn't use too much energy. An easily digestible meal makes content and sated, doesn't cause flatulence and fatigue after the meal. The perfect spices increase the healthiness of our meals. Very often, just small doses of herbs and spice will suffice. They are not used to make us sated, but to help our digestive organs to digest the food.

6.2 Recipes

The recipes list the ingredients to be used and the cooking instructions show how the dish is prepared. The list of ingredients shows the concerned quantities as well as the relevance for the therapy. If you find „omit", try to comply or find an alternative from the „list of recommended foodstuffs". Mostly it shall result just in a small change of taste when you simply avoid this ingredient.
Mild cooking methods: boiling, stewing, poaching, steaming
Strong cooking methods: barbecuing, roasting, frying, smoking
Balanced cooking methods: deep-frying, baking brick
Deep-freezing and warming in the microwave oven should be avoided (denaturalization).

6.3 Foodstuffs

Foodstuffs have an effect on body and soul like medicinal herbs, only a very much milder one. Dietary advice is mainly based on regional foodstuffs. The knowledge about the effects of each foodstuff and the knowledge, when which foodstuff shall be used, is based on the school medicine. Use ecologic-organic products, if possible. As everything should be cooked for a long time due to a better digestability and very rarely eaten raw, the food agrees with everyone.
The classification of the foodstuffs according to their effect on the body is the basis in order to achieve a harmonious status of health.
Dietary advisors do not recommend certain foodstuffs for everyone. The individual diet is tailor-made for the individual constitution.

Buy only fresh and ripe fruit and vegetables. You ought to leave unripe fruit and vegetables and such with brown spots and wilted leaves behind in the market. In this case take deep-frozen goods (never ready-to-serve dishes!). Fruit and vegetables are deep-frozen immediately after harvesting and often contain more vitamins and minerals than the goods from the vegetable shelf. Whereas conserved or tinned goods contain very much less biological substances. Also, salt, sugar and others are mostly added to the latter. Never leave the foodstuffs in the water after washing them to avoid that many vital substances get drowned. Clean salads, fruit and vegetables immediately before serving.

Please make sure of the hygienic processing of foodstuffs. Clean your salads, fruit and vegetables carefully. When cooking with meat, prepare all ingredients first and then process the meat products. Clean the worktop and tools very carefully. Wooden surfaces ought to be treated with a mild disinfectant regularly in order to reduce germination. Store fruit and vegetables separately, if possible. Harvested fruit and vegetables are still alive and emit e.g. ethylene gas, which makes other products ripen and age faster. Keep meat and fish in the closed packaging or store them in the fridge in closed containers.

6.4 Herbs

There are some basic rules for storing medicinal herbs. On principle, herbs must be protected from direct sunlight, humidity and heat.

Containers for the storage of herbs may be glasses, ceramic jars and even plastic containers. However, plastic is a rather unsuitable material and should only be a short-term solution. In case of glass containers, use a dark material.

Medicinal herbs cannot be kept for any long period. The shelf life of herbs is limited. However, it can be prolonged with suitable storage. The place should be dark, rather cool and absolutely dry. A wooden medicine cabinet, placed not directly next to a source of heat, would be ideal. Never buy large quantities of herbs so as not to have to throw them away. Label the container with the name of the herb and the date of harvesting or processing.

7 Other dietic-books

The following syndromes of dietetics, TCM or for a therapy supplement for cancer are available.

Dietetics

E001. Nutrition of the infant - baby food
E002. Nutrition during lactation
E003. Nutrition in old age
E004. Nutrition of children and adolescents
E005. Nutrition of athletes
E006. Light weight
E007. Pregnancy
E008. Full food

Protein and electrolyte - kidneys
E009. (hemodialysis) dialysis treatment
E010. Acute renal failure
E011. Chronic renal insufficiency
E012. Nephrotic syndrome
E013. Kidney stones (nephrolithiasis)

Gastrointestinal tract - pancreas
E014. Acute pancreatitis (inflammation of the pancreas)
E015. Chronic pancreatitis (inflammation of the pancreas)

Gastrointestinal tract - small intestine and large intestine
E016. Acute obstipation (constipation)
E017. Chronic obstipation (constipation)
E018. Colon irritabile
E019. Diverticulitis
E020. Acquired lactose intolerance (lactose malabsorption)
E021. Fructose malabsorption
E022. Glutensensitive enteropathy (celiac disease)
E023. Colectomy
E024. Short Bowel Syndrome

Gastrointestinal tract - liver, gallbladder, bile ducts
E025. Acute and chronic hepatitis (inflammation of the liver)
E026. Cholelithiasis (bile stones)
E027. fatty liver
E028. cirrhosis

Gastrointestinal tract - Stomach and duodenal intestine
E029. Acute gastritis
E030. Chronic gastritis
E031. Stomach bleeding
E032. Ulcus ventriculi and duodenal ulcer
E033. Condition after gastric surgery

Gastrointestinal tract - oral cavity and esophagus
E034. Stomatitis
E035. Esophageal carcinoma (esophageal cancer)
E036. Refluosophagitis (heartburn)

Special diseases
E037. Phenylketonuria (PKU)
E038. Rheumatic joint diseases

Metabolism
E039. Obesity (overweight)
E040. Diabetes mellitus
E041. Eating disorders (underweight)

Fat metabolism
E042. Hypercholesterolaemia (increased cholesterol level)
E043. Hepatic Encephalopathy

Heart and circulation
E044. Arteriosclerosis (arterial calcification)
E045. Heart insufficiency
E046. Hypertension
E047. Hyperuricaemia and gout

Changed nutrient requirements
E048. In case of fever
E049. For malignant diseases
E050. After burns
E051. Radiation and chemotherapy

CANCER
E100. Pancreatic cancer
E101. Bladder cancer
E102. Blood cancer (leukemia)
E103. Breast cancer
E104. Colorectal cancer
E105. Gastric cancer
E106. Kidney cancer
E107. Esophageal cancer

TCM
E200. Bladder - moisture heat in the bladder
E201. Bladder - moisture and cold in the bladder
E202. Bladder - emptiness and cold in the bladder
E203. Large intestine - external cold affects the large intestine
E204. Large intestine - moisture heat in the large intestine
E205. Large intestine - heat blocks the intestine II acute
E206. Large intestine - dryness of the colon
E207. Large intestine - Yang deficiency (cold)
E208. Heart - Blood insufficiency
E209. Heart - Blood stagnation
E210. Heart - Fire
E211. Heart - Hot mucus clogs the heart pores

E212. Heart - Cold mucus clogs the heart pores
E213. Heart - Qi deficiency
E214. Heart - Yang deficiency
E215. Heart - Yin deficiency
E216. Liver - Ascending Liver Yang
E217. Liver - Blood deficiency
E218. Liver - Blood stagnation
E219. Liver - Moisture heat in liver and gall bladder
E220. Liver - Fire
E221. Liver - Gall bladder Qi-Empty
E222. Liver - Cold in the liver meridian
E223. Liver - Qi stagnation
E224. Liver - Wind
E225. Liver - Wind with ascending liver Yang
E226. Liver - Wind with blood anemic
E227. Liver - Wind with extreme heat
E228. Lung - Qi deficiency
E229. Lung - Mucus-moisture in the lungs
E230. Lung - Mucus-heat in the lungs
E231. Lung - Mucus-cold in the lungs
E232. Lung - Dryness of the lungs
E233. Lung - Wind-heat attacks the lungs
E234. Lung - Wind-cold affects the lungs
E235. Lung - Yin deficiency
E236. Stomach - Bloodstagnation
E237. Stomach - Fire
E238. Stomach - Cold with liquid
E239. Stomach - Nutrition stagnation
E240. Stomach - Qi deficiency
E241. Stomach - Rebellious Qi
E242. Stomach - Yin Emptiness
E243. Spleen - Heat and moisture attack the spleen
E244. Spleen - Coldness and moisture affects the spleen
E245. Spleen - Qi deficiency
E246. Spleen - Qi deficiency + Declining spleen Qi
E247. Spleen - Qi deficiency + spleen does not control the blood
E248. Spleen - Yang deficiency
E249. Kidney - Heart and kidney no longer communicate
E250. Kidney - Jing deficiency
E251. Kidney - Kidneys cannot receive the Qi
E252. Kidney - Qi is not stable
E253. Kidney - Yang deficiency
E254. Kidney - Yin deficiency

For further information visit nutribook.info.

8   EBNS - Software for nutritional counseling

The main task of the database is to create personalized nutritional advice for each patient individually. The database was developed for Dietetics and Traditional Chinese Medicine.

The Database supports training and advices in the daily work routine.

The computer program provides lists of recipes, ingredients and herbs, which are given to the client. individually adjustable according to patient's request from whole food to vegetarians (lacto, ovo, ...). For every register there is an information sheet which can be given to the client. All texts can be individually designed.

The syndromes can be combined and result in an intersection of the recommended recipes and ingredients. The automated diagnosis for the TCM enables you to check your experience during the training as well as to confirm your diagnosis in the working day. You select several predefined symptoms and have the program automatically display the relevant syndromes.

How to work with the database:
Select the patient / client, select one or more of the syndromes you diagnosed and print the folder.

You can change all values, create new symptoms or syndromes, develop recipes, change or adapt ingredients and herbs to your findings. In simple client management, all relevant data about the person is stored. You get an overview of the past diagnoses and the development of the course of the disease.

As a consultant you save a lot of time when you print out the recipe, food and herbal lists for the recognized syndromes and give them to the clients. You can use this time for a personal conversation. With the database, dieticians and nutritionists can view the nutrients and trace elements for each recipe and develop recipes for syndromes even with suggested ingredients.

All recipe and grocery lists can also be ordered from me as a combination of several diseases. I wish all readers good luck, health and happiness in life.
More information can be found at www.ebns.at.
Volunteer: www.krebsinfo.at
Josef Miligui